A Startup Called Life

Knowledge about startups that can help you improve your life

Contents

INCEPTION
Chapter 1: The Idea
Chapter 2: Value and Market

SCALEUP
Chapter 3: Product-Market Fit (PMF)
Chapter 4: Branding: A Game of High Stakes
Chapter 5: Pivot: A New Beginning
Chapter 6: Retained Profits

EXIT
Chapter 7: The Exit

Chapter 1

The Idea

"The ideas that most people derided as ridiculous have produced the best outcomes"
~Fred Wilson

"If your idea can make lives simple, nothing can stop you. Nothing"
~ Unknown

It all begins with an idea. Maybe you thought of a great product which can impact millions, or want to use something that's already in one industry, in another industry, or have an additional improvement to one of the products already out there. Whatever be the case, you need to figure out your value proposition first. What is something that people are willing to pay you for? It could not just be for a business, it could also be a skill you've been honing, or pretty much anything. When something seems valuable enough, people are willing to pay a premium price for it. Luxurious cars are damn expensive, but people see value in it, so these companies still have regular and consistent sales.

Where value goes, money follows.
A common term you would have heard in the stock market is 'sector rotation'. Let's assume that pharma stocks have been performing well for the previous week for just about any reason. Out of the blue, the government announces a new policy in the IT sector which will revolutionize the whole industry. Since now the perceived value of this sector is higher, there will be a shift of capital (wealth) from the pharma stocks to the IT stocks. Thus, the people's money is 'rotating' about the industry sectors, and so is the potential value. This rotation could be daily, weekly, monthly etc. but usually follows a periodic regular pattern.

At the very beginning, an idea might sound stupid right off the bat. However, this isn't a factor in how much potential value it can give. I remember in one of the videos I saw, Marc Andreessen[1] says the two stupidest ideas people can think of, are living in someone else's house and giving out a part of your house to someone else. Airbnb mixed both these ideas into one platform, and is a billion-dollar business. The main thing about Airbnb is their timing was perfect. It was the 2008 housing crisis, and people sought out affordable options for everything. So even if the ideas may seem crazy, if the time is right, anything can happen. Before the pandemic, Zoom was only used for international meetings or when it wasn't possible for everyone to come together. When the virus broke out, everyone was at home and people couldn't come together at all. And thus, Zoom's valuation rose and it became one of the top companies by valuation. Timing is important. However, there's no way to predict the perfect time to launch a particular product. As the saying goes, "The best time to plant a tree was 20 years ago. The second best time is now" The best time to start a company was 10 years ago. It would've become a unicorn, and maybe even a profitable one. The second best time to start a company is now.

Your idea may not be unique, it can also be an extended version of an already existing product. Google wasn't the first search engine, and Facebook wasn't the first social platform. Yet, they are at the top of their fields because they brought something to the table that their competitors couldn't. If you have an idea, chances are, there are close to 5 other teams already working on it. You can outdo your competition by either working harder, or by thinking out of the box using innovative methods. Working hard is important, but there is a ceiling to it. You can only work so much in a week before getting burnt out. Innovation, on the other hand, gets the job done in much lesser time and literally has no limit to it! Here's where unfair advantages come in.

An unfair advantage is something which you have, that the others don't. This could be in any field, in any way. In the book *Shortcut Your Startup*[2], the authors mention that unfair advantages 'compress time'. The example they give is to imagine you're competing with Jessica Alba's company[3]. To get your product out there, you would have to cold-call multiple firms, magazines, get your social media game going, and so on. While all of this would take at least 3-4 months, Jessica, on the other hand, could get word out to her 25 million social media followers at the click of a button. This is how unfair advantages can help you compress and save time using leverage. And in a startup, time is absolutely precious. You just cannot waste time on unimportant activities during the initial stages of a startup. The book also mentions that customers nowadays don't think twice before switching to another product fulfilling the same needs.

Here's an excerpt from the book:

"Increased switching rates are one reason that it's important to compress time through unfair advantages. In the United States, companies are struggling to retain customers, as the birthrate of new and better companies has increased. We now exist in a switching economy in which the amount of potential revenue that switches has skyrocketed."

People don't hesitate to switch between products and services nowadays. With the wide array of options available, all the power lies with the customer. It may look like a zero-sum game, but in reality it isn't. We see newer companies emerging everyday, and each of them have a share of the market. There's always more room at the top, and anyone can get there. Unfair advantages propel you and make the journey easier.

Unfair advantages not only compress time, but also give you an idea of where your strengths lie. The field in which your unfair advantage lies is the field in which you must push and work on the most. While playing to your strengths is a great strategy, but in startups, the chain is as strong as its weakest link. So when you're pushing the most in one field, make sure that you're at least doing the bare minimum in other fields.

An interesting point is that the college that you go to or the one that you graduated from might also be an unfair advantage. One of the main reasons people want to get into good colleges is the environment, exposure and networking opportunities that you get by just being there. Good colleges attract the top talent from around the country and the world, and these people will be your friends on and off campus. The alumni network of these colleges is just as great, and you can get in touch with some extraordinary people. Coming from a good college also gives you a sense of accomplishment, both internally and externally. If the institute has a low acceptance rate and you still made it, that is an accomplishment which will be with you throughout your life. It becomes much easier to forge new connections and find new partners when you're from one of the best colleges. People also have a huge amount of respect for you, no matter what happens later on in your life.

While talking to my dad in my early teens, he told me this one thing which I remember to date. He said whatever happens in the world, there is one thing which will always have demand - food. And good quality food, at that. No matter what catastrophe hits the planet, no matter what kind of recession it is, this field will always flock people and attention. And money, of course.

If you think about it, hunger is the one thing that can never be satiated once and for all.

No matter how much you eat now, you will eventually feel hungry again. What you eat and how much you eat depends on your culture and milieu, but the basic fact which unites all of humanity is that we all feel hungry from time to time. Any business which aims at resolving the problem of hunger, technically has infinite demand!

The McDonald brothers[4], Richard, and Maurice, wanted to be in the film industry, so they took up odd jobs at Columbia Pictures. They saved enough money and opened a small theatre of their own. In 1929. Couldn't be a worse time. People didn't have enough to get by, so who would want to go watch movies? Nobody on their street was making money, except for one man. That man owned a hot dog and root beer stand. Even if there's an economic recession, people still gotta eat, right? So the brothers set up their own food stall, and over 90 years later a McDonald's burger is something each of us looks forward to.

Before you get too excited about this and think you have the next unicorn, I have to tell you, it isn't that simple. Though the demand is technically infinite, there are a lot of things to consider. As an idea, any food business is great. But the world doesn't reward ideas, it rewards execution. And that's where most companies, not just food ones, go wrong. Every business idea is great, but the execution is what separates the best from the rest. You can have an amazing idea but no execution, or could have an idea nobody thinks is great but somehow execute it to perfection. I could go on and give examples, but I think you get the point.

Like I said, it all begins with an idea. And the idea behind this book is that almost all components of a startup have their own parallels or counterparts in our everyday lives, it's just that we can't see them clearly. Our life can technically be associated to that of a business, and many aspects of the two can be correlated. Imagine if you, as a person, were a company, and the product going out into the world was you. You are the managing director, CEO, and also an employee in this corporation. If everything is going well, everybody's celebrating. If things are going rough, you need to take up responsibility for your own actions. Hopefully by the end of this book you will learn the importance of the small actions and their repercussions in your life, and your mind will open up to newer possibilities and ways of thinking. With the help of this book, I hope you make your book (your life) better and more enriching. This isn't just for startup enthusiasts, it's for anyone who wants a different perspective on life. You will, hopefully, learn a bit about startups, but that isn't the main objective.

At the end of the day, it is, after all, your book. Go ahead and take notes, highlight stuff, scribble stuff, skip sentences, paragraphs, pages, chapters, do anything you want! Have a blast :)

Chapter 2

Value and Market

"Try not to be a man of success, but a man of value"
~ Albert Einstein

"Value is more expensive than price"
~ Unknown

In every money-making venture, be it creating an app, selling vada pav, making music, or even writing a book, there is an exchange of value. The world doesn't run on money, it runs on value. Think about this - the 10 rupee and 2000 rupee notes are made from basically the same paper, and are of almost the same dimensions, but one is worth 200 times the other. Why is it that two things which are so similar have such a big difference in their value?

This is because in the system we humans have created, we associate certain types of notes with a lesser value, and other types with more value. If the note looks a certain way, and has a particular barcode and texture, its value is perceived. This is also why branding is important. More on that in the next chapter.

Random new topic starts

The Nixon Shock of 1971 changed quite a lot. Richard Nixon, the President of the USA suspended the interconversion of USD to gold. This was done to promote creation of jobs, and to protect the dollar from money speculators, internationally. Post the Vietnam War, Nixon wanted to reduce the average cost of living in America, and thus took these measures. It marked the end of the Bretton Woods Agreement which had started after the Second World War. I don't know much about this agreement, but Investopedia does, so I'm going to cite it here:

"The Bretton Woods Agreement revolved around the external values of foreign currencies. Fixed versus the U.S. dollar, the value of foreign currencies was expressed in gold at a price determined by Congress. However, a dollar surplus imperiled the system in the 1960s. At the time, the U.S. did not have enough gold to cover the volume of dollars circulating throughout the world. That led to an overvaluation of the dollar."

So that was the Bretton Woods Agreement. What Nixon essentially did was separate the value of the US Dollar and commodities such as gold. This changed the fundamentals of the US economy and had an effect on countries worldwide. For further knowledge, visit the link[5] at the end of the book.

Random new topic ends

For any commercial endeavor, you need an audience. This audience has a want or a need that you are somehow fulfilling through your products or services. Sometimes this audience (the market) might not have such a need, and this is one of the main reason that 35% of startups fail[6]. Market research is one of the most important things any startup must do at the beginning to get a fair idea of the market, also known as a 'market pulse' – this factor can often decide the survival of a company.

It is important to note that your target market cannot include everybody. For instance, Facebook could've easily said that their product is basically for everyone and anyone can use it, but they scaled up strategically, going from college to college. This is similar to how Clubhouse also expanded, using the limited number of invites. The initial set of users, in both cases, were the ones who took the products forward by recommending it to their friends and family.

As Peter Thiel puts it,
"Network effects can be powerful, but you'll never reap them unless your product is valuable to its very first users when the network is necessarily small"

When this network is small, the first few users have to be absolutely impressed by the product. They then become your marketing agents, and go around recommending the product to their near and dear ones. Even the ones who don't like the product can help, because they can give feedback, which is ever so critical in a startup.

Kevin Kelly has written a book called "1,000 true fans" which is about how creators should approach building a community[6]. Once you have gained a thousand loyal die-hard customers, there's nothing and nobody who can stop you. It may take some time to gather these thousand fans, but the payoff is worth the wait. It is important to note that your thousand true fans will buy anything you put out into the market, because they are deeply connected with the values and philosophy behind you and your products. These thousand odd fans are people who will follow you on every social media platform, buy all your merch, and watch all of your content.

One of the main ways to reach this thousand true fans milestone is through word-of-mouth marketing. If you have a great product/service that's positively impacting the lives of users, there's no reason why these users wouldn't recommend it to their friends and family. As this chain grows, you start getting more and more unique customers with a unique experience of your product/service. In today's day and age, the easiest way to communicate with others is social media. At the click of a button, you can send a picture or a video to thousands of people out there. This level of broadcasting, that too for free, is a boon at the hands of creators. I understand that social media has its own pitfalls as well, but it was fundamentally designed to be a good thing, helping people connect and share their ideas. This is also the most easily obtainable unfair advantage (throwback to chapter 1) because you can get followers for free, and usually quite quickly.

Another important aspect of social media is how it can help you validate. Whether it's a new product you want to launch or a song that you've been writing, you can show the world a small glimpse of it and see the response. However, you need to sometimes take these responses with a pinch of salt. There are hundreds of people out there ready to pull you down, and social media has a ton of them. So before you start crying over the negative comments or less number of likes, just know that a lot of this is by people who just want to demotivate you. It is always advisable to have a trusted group of people with whom you can share new ideas and look for feedback. I call this group "The Guinea Pigs". Whenever I have an idea about anything, be it a new song, a book or even a standup set, I run it by this group of people. They give me honest feedback and I love it. When the idea of this book popped into my head, this was the first thing I did. The response was mixed, but mostly leaning towards the green signal. Thus, the journey began.

If there's one thing I want you to take away from this chapter, it's that no matter what you are selling or creating, always try to add value to people's lives. This value can be in the form of anything. It could be being kind to everybody you meet, it could be giving a beggar money, or even teaching your brother a skill. And as much as possible, give more than you take. I know this sounds like a stupid or a fairytale notion, but trust me, it works, and will help you in the long run.

Chapter 3

Product-Market Fit (PMF)

"The only thing that matters is getting product market fit"
~ Marc Andreessen

"Before product market fit, your only job that matters is to build a great product"
~ Sam Altman

This chapter is probably the most random thing that has ever occurred to me. Try not to laugh and please don't get offended or anything, this is just my viewpoint. You can probably skip this chapter and go straight to the next one. Or you can read it and finish the book in its entirety like a chad. Gigachad. Ok I'll stop. So without any further ado, let's get started.

Businesses strive to reach a stage known as product market fit or PMF. According to Marc Andreessen, product-market fit basically means finding a good market with a product capable of satisfying that market. This important milestone is a shared responsibility of all departments of the business. There are many ways in which an organization can achieve product market fit. You can change the market, change the product, change the branding, change the values associated, or even start afresh (quite similar to the pivot, chapter 5) The point of a pivot is to reach the PMF stage. PMF is considered a very important milestone from the venture capitalist point of view. Investors give utmost importance to this stage, because it is almost a sure-shot way of predicting if a business can succeed going forward. It usually takes a while to reach PMF, but it's worth the wait.

There are no set of metrics which can tell you if you have achieved PMF, but there

are a few ways to assess whether you're getting there. Some of the characteristics of PMF are:
- Demand for the product skyrockets
- Sales cycles are short
- Word of mouth marketing is happening
- No time for improving the product
- Huge need to hire talent

One of the ways you can know that you are getting there is user feedback. If users are happy with what they have, then you should be a millionaire. If not, well, get to work :) Feedback tells you what's working, what's not, and where there's room for improvement. It could be the color, a small feature, or even the entire product itself (time to pivot). Based on the feedback received, you can figure out how far you are from PMF. Like I said earlier, it takes time, and loads of effort, but the payoff is worth it.

Now comes the relation to everyday life. All of us in life require physical and emotional stability, for which we look for partners. People spend a lot of time looking for 'the one' who they will spend the rest of their lives with. Finding this one special person may take a day, a week or a lifetime. But when you find that one person, you know for sure. Before I start going all romantic and weird, (some say cute, others say weird) let me get to the point I'm trying to make. The bond between a product and the market need is very similar to the bond between two people in a relationship. And I don't mean every relationship, I mean that special one which you have only once in your life.

Everybody has flaws, imperfections and whatnot. But that one person doesn't mind. Finding the right person will elevate your life, and give you the things your heart desires at the same time. This person will open doors which you never knew existed, and will be one of the big factors in your success.

There are 2 important decisions you make in your life. The first one is the work that you do, or what puts food on the table. The second one is who you spend your life with. Both of these decisions more or less shape your entire life. As Tim Ferriss (and many other people) say in the book Tools of Titans[7], "How you do one thing is how you do everything". So these important decisions not only shape your entire life but also affect many other small decisions you make along the way as well, so it is very important to think them through.

The relation of PMF to everyday life does not just stop at that one special and unique once-in-a-lifetime relationship. PMF could be between a mentor and a mentee, between a salesman and his clients, between two best friends, or between any set of people.

I had to shift cities during my childhood, and had to find the set of people who I had a perfect fit with. It took a while, but it was worth it.

It is important to cherish each and every relationship, because life is indeed short. This obviously doesn't mean that you keep all the toxic relationships alive as well, just learn when to tow the line.

This chapter was inspired by many incidents that occurred over a span of 4 months, and proved that I have indeed found that special someone. My amazing brain then somehow related that to PMF, and tada. If you felt this chapter was an utter waste, I'm sorry. But it is what it is.

Chapter 4

Branding: A Game of High Stakes

"Your brand is the single most important investment you can make in your business"
~Steve Forbes

"People respond to how we're dressed"
~Harvey Specter

Jeff Bezos[8] has famously said *"A brand for a company is like a reputation for a person"*. And that's exactly what this chapter is about. The classic definition of branding is 'the promotion of a particular product or company by means of advertising and distinctive design'.

Why is branding important?

Let's take the example of a software product. Just as the back-end is important because it has the main algorithms and servers, the front-end or the UI (user interface) is just as important because that is what the customers see and interact with. In a startup, your product/service, team, and business models are important, but if the customer doesn't like the look of the product or doesn't have a good experience with it, then it's pointless. A movie can have the greatest director, amazing actors, and a stellar crew. But if the end product isn't liked by the masses, then it's all in vain. Or maybe the movie itself might be great, but if the posters or the trailer aren't liked by people, it's going to fail.

A brand is the exterior. People still judge books by their covers (you judged this one didn't you) so it's important that the first impression a customer gets of your brand is a good and lasting one. The internet and social media make it easy to get impressions on a large number of customers. This can be both positive and negative. Due to social media it is now easier than ever to reach a million people, and also to spread rumours and fake news among the masses. Due to the vast number of media outlets and websites, people have a hard time figuring out what is true and what isn't. This is why having a strong and reputed brand image is of utmost importance.

Imagine a rumour comes up tomorrow that your company is involved in some illegal affairs. The average person who has no clue about your company is going to get a negative first impression of the business, and might not ever become a customer! But if there's someone who truly believes in what your brand stands for, then he knows that this is just a rumour and would still be loyal to you. Even if you do end up doing some unlawful or shady affairs (please don't) this loyal customer will understand the rationale (what rationale do you need to commit crimes?). Point being, have loyal customers. It helps.

A study by three MIT scholars found that fake news travels six times faster than legit news[9]. Though there's no way to prevent fake news from spreading, as an organization you can make an effort to protect your interests by showcasing your core values and principles. This is one of the reasons the culture of a business is so important. If from the inception stage the management imbibes a culture of honesty and integrity in the members, the company attracts more and better talent, improves its offerings, and thus makes more profits. And as I have mentioned ahead, as within, so without. So if you have better people on the inside, you will naturally attract honest and loyal customers.

Values are the 'why' of a business. And as Simon Sinek says, Start With Why[13]. The values and motivations of employees as well as managers is integral to the company's success, just as much as anything else. It is important to value the image of the employees as well, because they represent your company out there. They technically have a brand of their own, and their own needs and interests.

At the core of every economic (money-making) activity is sales. No matter what your job is or which industry you are a part of, some part of your job involves selling something. And in sales, first impressions take up a much more important role. If you want to make somebody buy your product or service, you need to think long-term. If you decide that a particular customer is not worth spending too much time on, then you are gravely mistaken. As Dr. David Schwartz[10] puts it, *"Put service first and money takes care of itself"*. This essentially means that if your primary intention is to serve and improve the lives of people, you will not have financial problems for most of your life. However, if you go running behind money and do not aim at improving the lives of people in some fashion, money will continue to elude you.

Yes, tangent, I know. Coming back to branding. There's a reason companies spend millions of dollars every year in marketing and ad campaigns. One of the main reasons is to get the word out there, and make sure people are aware of the company and its offerings. They want to get through the obscurity and make sure that their company's message gets through to the masses.

I once saw a video or something (I think I read about it, not sure) in which they say that the internet is like a vast desert, and when you put yourself out there through social media, or any other way, you're putting footprints on that desert. So the more footprints you have, the easier it is for people to find you online. Some of these footprints are small, some are big. Your aim as a company should be to put out as many footprints online as well as offline to show a strong presence.

If you think about it, you have a brand yourself. You have a product (you), a reputation, a net worth, and so on. Like in a company, you too get to decide what your brand (your name, in this case) stands for and what it signifies. Even if you lose money, your house, your car, everything else, you will always have your name and reputation with you. There will be people out there trying to bring you down, but it is your job to keep your head high and face them with a smile. There's a beautiful quote by Chris Colfer[11] which goes: *"When people hurt you over and over, think of them like sandpaper. They may scratch and hurt you a bit, but in the end, you end up polished and they end up useless"*

In one of the books I read, I'm not sure which one, there's a concept of internal elections. Every time you behave in a certain way, you are in a sense voting for that kind of personality. If you helped someone on the way, then your vote goes to the helpful personality inside you. If you smoke, then that is also a vote to your personality. So on, all your actions essentially vote for one of your character traits. In the end, your personality is a mixture of all of these actions. Your actions determine the voting, and in turn, determine your character.

In the movie '13 Hours' there's a quote by Joseph Campbell[12] which goes *"All the gods, all the heavens, all the hells are within you"*. I cried when I heard that. No clue why. The quote just proves that everything external we see is an extension or a counterpart of something that is internal.

As the saying goes, *"As within, so without"*. What you think of yourself greatly affects how others perceive you. If you have a very good opinion about yourself and hold yourself in high regard, the world will follow. Your body language and posture dictates to a great extent what you think of yourself and how the world holds you. Your outward appearance and the company you keep around you also affect your personal brand and image. Though people get cancelled for judging and stuff, a vast majority of the population still does judge you from the exterior. So look the part, be confident, and don't be too worried about the outcome. Of anything.

Chapter 5

Pivot: A New Beginning

"Pivoting is not the end of the disrupting process, but the beginning of the next leg of your journey"

~Jay Samit

"What feels like the end is often the beginning"

~ Unknown

Pivoting is the process in which a startup changes its business strategy in one or many areas. It is essentially done to accommodate changes in the business environment. As the business environment is dynamic and ever-changing, it is absolutely essential for entrepreneurs to stay alert about local and global news. The concept of pivoting is more common with people following the 'lean startup' methodology. It has been mentioned in various books, and people have mixed opinions about it.

That's cool and all, but what's the lean startup methodology?
According to universitylabpartners.org, *"The lean startup methodology is a method of managing and building a business or startup by experimenting, testing, and iterating while developing products based on findings from your tests and feedback."*

Easy, right? Keep experimenting, keep iterating until you hit that sweet spot. This sweet spot is called product-market fit, as mentioned in chapter 3. The point is, this methodology teaches you how to navigate a startup. Tells you when to accelerate, when to slow down, and when to change lanes. If you want to know more, you can read *The Lean Startup*[14] by Eric Ries.

A pivot can be of many types. You might want to pivot on a particular part of your business idea, or might want to refurbish the entire company altogether. You might zoom in on one particular feature of your product which people love the most, or you might zoom out, and make an entire product into just a small feature of a larger product. You can change the customer segment, marketing platform, growth strategy, or even the basic technology behind the product. No matter what kind of pivot you undertake, the basic idea is that there is a big change in the business. Either something which wasn't working is shut down, or something which was working is expanded.

Sometimes in life, all seems lost. It feels like the thing you've been working so hard for was never meant to be yours, and it was just a carrot on a stick. You tried, you failed, you tried again, but it just didn't happen. To share an anecdote, I took part in the Breakthrough Junior Challenge for 3 years in a row, and was nowhere close to the top. If you look at the videos though, you'll see that there was little to no value in them. This entire journey taught me a very important lesson which I shared in the 'value and market' chapter - always add value. The point I'm making is, failure always brings with it a lesson. There's a line I love to say, and it goes *"Failure is only useless if you didn't learn something new"*.

Another important lesson I learnt from the competition experience is that doing your best often has nothing to do with succeeding. I know that sounds bleak and hopeless and makes you want to quit, but it's true. Your best level might be someone else's average level, and yet someone else's starting point. This is why success is not guaranteed to anybody at anytime. This is also why it is so important to keep pushing yourself and your limits.

There are times when you feel like you had it all figured out, it was all going to work out, you were almost there. But then it all comes crashing down. Wiped away. Clean slate. But what you think is a catastrophe might just be an opportunity in disguise. What if you're made for something bigger and better? What if your slate was congested and needed a little breathing space and the only way was to clear it completely? The old makes way for the new. As the saying goes, there is opportunity in the midst of chaos. Don't be afraid of starting afresh, be afraid of staying still. That's a good line. I'm not sure if someone's written that before, but yes.

In almost every inspirational journey, there is an inflection point. At that point, the protagonist's life hits rock bottom. Things could go much worse, and the person knows this. The past hasn't been kind, and there's no guarantee the future will be either. This person has two choices - he/she can sulk and complain about the situation and circumstances and how bad things only happen to him/her, or, take responsibility for his/her life and make sure that the same mistakes aren't repeated. If you hit rock bottom, it's only going to get better from there.

On 25th December 2021, I gave my first full-length JEE Main mock test. Up until then, I was pretty confident about my preparation. Turns out, I wasn't prepared at all. In the test I gave, I got negative marks. Negative. Out of 300. That was rock bottom. I could've given up on the JEE dream and sat and sulked and gotten nowhere, but I chose to fight back. It was too late to apply to universities abroad by then, so I had to continue with the chosen path. There's no such thing as failure, only feedback. That turned out to be my inflection point. The inflection point of a graph is where the slope changes its sign. My slope was going negative, and I made it positive (see, that's funny, because I got negative marks, and tested positive for

COVID a month later). I had to rethink how I was studying and start over. The phrase usually is 'start from scratch' but I was technically below the zero level.

And here I am today, after clearing JEE Mains. *It ain't much, but it's honest work.*

There were times when I felt like it's worthless, and a few days when I had suicidal thoughts as well. There were ups and downs, rough patches and smooth patches, but now here we are at the end. It wasn't easy, but it was worth it. And that's what I feel life is all about. It isn't easy, but worth it.

My support system is the best in the world. I could talk to people who had different versions of the same experience. This was very helpful because having a different perspective of the same thing is very important and gives you and interesting set of views. It also teaches you which pitfalls to avoid and which areas to focus more on.

So whenever you are thinking about your support system, try to get as many different viewpoints as possible.

One of the biggest lessons I learned during this process was dealing with failure. I gave around 10 competitive exams in total, and a lot of them didn't go according to the plan. I couldn't perform upto my full potential, but there's nothing I could do about it after the exam. If you are batting at 99 runs and get bowled, there's nothing you can do about it. Yes there will be regrets, but you just have to keep your chin up, face the critics, conquer the regret, and move on. A wise man doesn't cry over spoilt milk, he just makes cottage cheese and moves on. And that's what you do in every situation. Give your best, hope for the best, but if the result doesn't come your way it's alright. You might have bigger things and better opportunities in the future.

If you start over now, there will be a few differences than when you began first. Your experience, learnings, network, familiarity, and whatnot. You may want to start a business, write a book, sing a song, or do anything in the world. All you need is that first step. Don't look at the tip of the mountain, look at base camp. You have to get there first. Like the sherpas, there will always be people around to guide you and help you get to the destination, but in the end, you can get the horse to the pond, but if it isn't thirsty, it won't drink the water.

It's the determination and willpower which will eventually push you towards the goal. There will be setbacks, there will be tough times, but they are only there to make sure that you are worthy enough of the end result. These challenges build your personality, and shape you into the kind of person who deserves the goal. They test your patience and make sure that you are leveling up not just physically but also mentally. They say success is a journey, not a destination. So it's also important to enjoy the process of leveling up. If you detest the process and do it just for the sake of it, the end result might not satisfy you as much.

Chapter 6

Retained Profits

"If you don't find a way to make money while you sleep, you will have to work until you die"
~Warren Buffett

"Money isn't the most important thing in life, but it's reasonably close to oxygen on the 'gotta have it' scale"
~ Zig Ziglar

In 12th grade Business Studies, we have a chapter called "Sources of Finance". In the chapter, one of the internal sources mentioned is known as retaining or 'ploughing back' of profits. I loved this concept so much that I decided to dedicate a whole chapter to it :)

Companies across the world require capital (money) for various reasons, be it expanding, staying alive for the next few months, repaying debt, or any other reason. And they raise this capital via a multitude of financial sources. Sources of finance for a company are broadly divided into 2 categories, internal (owned funds) and external (borrowed funds). Internal sources include money invested by the founder, selling of assets and retained profits. External sources include loans, venture capitalists and bank overdrafts. Some of these funds may be raised for long periods of time while others are raised only for a short period.

Companies prefer to go for internal sources of business finance due to various reasons. Some of them are:
- There is more control, and no repayment commitments
- It limits the influence of outsiders in the company

- There is no additional cost such as interest, tax etc
- You don't have to issue additional equity

Internal sources of finance are also known as owned funds, and the phrase itself tells you that the funds are already owned by the company. Thus it is a safer and more trustworthy source of funds than borrowed funds.

As mentioned, one of the internal sources is retained profits, and here's the textbook explanation for the same:

"Retained earnings or ploughing back of profits refers to the process of retaining a part of the net profit year after year and reinvesting the same in business. This source is also called 'self-financing' as it is an internal method of finance. Retained profits are a popular source of capital for modernisation and expansion of business."

Self-financing. I love the phrase. It is the best way of sustainable long-term financing. This is one of the most important steps the people in our country need to take if we want to become a self-reliant nation. As long as our population is dependent on organizations and corporate firms to create jobs and feed them, there is going to be a disparity. There are only so many jobs out there, but the population is growing everyday. Our country already faces a severe shortage of jobs, and with technology developing at breakneck speed, this might only worsen.

Ok I went off on a tangent there. Coming back to retained profits (also known as retained earnings).

The amount of profits that a company can retain or plough back depends on a few factors:
- ☐ More the net profits, greater is the capacity to retain them

- The plans that the company has about the future in terms of expansion and modernisation have an important influence
- The age of the company is also a big factor
- The dividend policy of the organization dictates to what extent the profits can be ploughed back

Relating this amazing concept to personal finance, if we can somehow partake a small amount from our income/salary and put it in either an investment instrument or a side hustle, there would be a steady inflow of capital to fuel your dream, save up for retirement, or whatever else you want to do with that money. Just like companies, people also require capital for various reasons. It could be a vacation, your child's college tuition, or even to buy a PS5 (feel free to gift me one). It could serve as an emergency fund in case something untoward happens. It could be exactly what you need when you see an opportunity and want to grab it. I mean, a little extra money doesn't hurt, right?

Tearing a page from Robert Kiyosaki's teachings, you would want to use this retained profit to build or create assets. What are assets? Simply put, assets put money into your pocket while liabilities remove money from your pocket. No matter at which stage of life you are in, your primary focus should be to increase your net inflow by creating assets which give you an additional income. The income generated by these assets is known as passive income or side income. This side income is what you should be using to purchase the dream car, or the dream house, because this money is independent of what you earn from your job/profession. Eventually, there will come a time when the side income exceeds your primary income, and that is when you make the jump. You're no longer an employee. There's no boss, no time restrictions, more happiness, more freedom, and you are now free to live life on your own terms.

It is to be noted that the goal to be attained is freedom, and money is merely just a tool to get you there. The freedom you have when you can buy anything you want because it now fits your budget. The freedom to travel anywhere. The freedom to spend more time with your loved ones.

Another related concept is that of a "money tree". We've all heard the saying that money doesn't grow on trees, but this concept is pretty cool. Imagine you have an investment which you've been 'watering' for a while now, it will eventually grow and bear fruit. After a while, even if you stop watering this tree, it will continue to absorb water and nutrients by itself and give you whatever it has to offer. It is a sustainable and long-term idea, which needs a certain amount of time before it starts fully flourishing and giving you desired results. A small price to pay for salvation. The unspoken fact, however, is that trees can suffer harm in many ways. Not enough water, too much water, forest fires, diseases, whatnot. The point is that there is a huge amount of risk involved in such investment instruments. You can probably choose to withdraw your initial amount and let the remainder multiply itself just as a hedge against risks. There's a payoff between playing it safe and getting larger returns.

Time usually is a big factor in secondary wealth creation. Whether through mutual fund SIPs or general trading and investing, or in starting up a business, it takes a while before you start rolling in the big bucks. As Warren Buffett[16] said, "No matter how great the talent or efforts, some things just take time.". In the compound interest formula, the 'T' is the most important variable, because it is at the exponential level. It decides pretty much everything, so stay patient. One interesting thing about time is that the earlier you start saving and investing, the lesser money you need to buy one day of freedom in the future. Of course, there's inflation, geopolitical stuff and whatnot, but it's still true.

Another important point is that passive income is usually and mostly should be a secondary income. Your primary income must still come from your job or whatever you do to earn money currently. This is because creating a passive income stream is a risky and time-consuming process. As Harj Taggar said in Startup School 2022[17], *"don't drop out of college unless your side project becomes big"*. This advice is important because it's always safe to have a backup, no matter what. Though a lot of people believe that you should 'burn the boats' and go all in, I don't really like that idea.

Chapter 7

The Exit

"I always invest in companies an idiot could run, because one day one will"
~ Warren Buffett

"A king's time as ruler rises and falls like the sun. One day, the sun will set on my time here, and will rise with you as the new king"
~ Mufasa

"The only exit strategy is legacy"
~ Unknown

Everything that is created, gets destroyed. Every creature born on this planet has to depart one day. There comes a time when you have built your company to such a stage that it doesn't need you as an active component anymore. At this juncture, you have a multitude of choices. You can stay, and expand the organization further, you can sell it off to a larger multinational corporation, you can retire and hand over the reins to your successor, or do pretty much anything else. The point I'm making is that the exit is inevitable, yet to a small extent in our control.

You might want to still continue as the head of the company but age, health or any other factor might be a hindrance. Deciding who your successor will be is a mighty big task, because this is something you have built from scratch and don't want someone to run it to the ground. If you have done a good job with the operations and systems within the organization, then even the simplest of men will be able to run it smoothly and you won't have a hard time picking someone to take over. However, if due to whatever reasons, the company isn't there yet and still has a lot to accomplish, this decision must be made wisely. You may either pick someone on merit or by experience, but each method has its pros and cons. A rookie with top-notch skills and flair might not have the wisdom, and someone with grey hair might not have the skills anymore (No offense to people with grey hair).

The act of handing over your company to someone else is emotionally jarring and more bitter than sweet. However, it is how everything in the universe functions, and thus is inevitable. I remember in 2021 I was in a Clubhouse room with Dr. Velumani, the founder of Thyrocare. He had recently sold a part of the company to PharmEasy, and was talking about the journey and the exit. He related his emotions to that of a bride's father. He raised the child for years together, through good times and bad, and in the end he had to give it to someone else. Though the decision was his, there was still some amount of regret and sadness at the time. Letting go of something that you have loved and cherished for years is by no means easy, but at times required. That being said, it is time for me to let go of this book and I hope you enjoyed reading it :)

If you're feeling demotivated and stuff and need that quick dose of inspiration, here goes nothing:

Everything that you want exists. And it exists right outside of your comfort zone. Grab all the opportunities lying in front of you, and make the most of them. Become an unstoppable force in your field and industry. You got this. It's about time you started scripting your own history.
If Leicester City can win the Premier League, a bunch of Indians who nobody believed in can beat the mighty West Indies and win the World Cup, and a dog can go to space, then why the hell can't you do anything that you put your mind to?

God, I hate goodbyes. I had to shift cities thrice for multiple reasons, and it got harder with time. New friends, new environment, new experiences. There was always something to look forward to, but also something to reminisce about. So without further ado, here's the end of my first book and hopefully the start to many more.

Links

1. https://a16z.com/author/marc-andreessen/
2. https://amzn.to/3ybhYGV
3. https://www.honest.com
4. http://www.laalmanac.com/history/hi708.php
5. https://history.state.gov/milestones/1969-1976/nixon-shock
6. https://amzn.to/3TbDun1
7. https://amzn.to/3SCsAqc
8. https://www.forbes.com/profile/jeff-bezos/?sh=69d115441b23
9. https://news.mit.edu/2018/study-twitter-false-news-travels-faster-true-stories-0308
10. https://en.wikipedia.org/wiki/David_J._Schwartz_(motivational_writer)
11. https://en.wikipedia.org/wiki/Chris_Colfer

12. https://jcf.org/

13. https://amzn.to/3EezIVn

14. https://amzn.to/3SVYbCW

15. https://www.richdad.com/

16. https://www.forbes.com/profile/warren-buffett/?sh=762cdd074639

17. https://tinyurl.com/startupschool2022

www.ingramcontent.com/pod-product-compliance
Lightning Source LLC
Chambersburg PA
CBHW071121240526
45465CB00022B/737